Snap books®

GREEN CRAFTS

Cool Crafts
with
Old CDs

by Carol Sirrine

green projects for **Resourceful Kids**

CAPSTONE PRESS
a capstone imprint

Snap Books are published by Capstone Press,
151 Good Counsel Drive, P.O. Box 669, Mankato, Minnesota 56002.
www.capstonepress.com

Printed in the United States of America in North Mankato, Minnesota.
092009
005618CGS10

 Books published by Capstone Press are manufactured with paper
containing at least 10 percent post-consumer waste.

Library of Congress Cataloging-in-Publication Data
Sirrine, Carol.
Cool crafts with old CDs : green projects for resourceful kids / by Carol Sirrine.
    p. cm. — (Snap books. Green crafts)
    Includes bibliographical references and index.
    Summary: "Step-by-step instructions for crafts made from old CDs and information about
reusing and recycling" — Provided by publisher.
    ISBN 978-1-4296-4007-7 (library binding)
    1. Plastics craft — Juvenile literature. 2. Compact discs — Juvenile literature. 3. Salvage
(Waste, etc.) — Juvenile literature. I. Title.
TT297.S48 2010
745.58'4 — dc22   2009035404

Editor: Kathryn Clay
Designer: Juliette Peters
Production Specialist: Laura Manthe
Photo Stylist: Sarah Schuette
Project Production: Marcy Morin

Photo Credits:
All photos by Capstone Studio/Karon Dubke except:
Carol Sirrine with Liam, 32; Shutterstock/Amy Johansson (chain link fence design element);
Shutterstock/Ian O'Hanlon (recycling stamp design element)

Capstone Press thanks ArtStart in St. Paul, Minnesota, for its contributions
to the projects included in this book.

Essential content terms are **bold** and are defined at the bottom of the page
where they first appear.

Table of Contents

Introduction

Look around your home, in the car, or at school. Notice how many times you see someone popping a CD into a CD player or a computer. Since 1983 the compact disc has been an easy and cheap way to store information. However, this small storage system can be a big problem for the environment. Each month almost 50 tons (45 metric tons) of CDs are tossed into **landfills**. That's the weight of 15 elephants!

CD Safety

Some CDs, like music CDs, have a protective layer that makes them thicker and harder to cut. Burnable discs are thinner and easier to cut. When possible, use burnable discs for projects that involve cutting CDs.

Cutting a CD creates sharp pieces. Remember to wear safety glasses to protect your eyes. You may also want to wear gardening gloves when handling CD pieces.

landfill — an area where garbage is stacked and covered with dirt

CD Colors

CDs are made from plastic and coated with a thin layer of metal. This coating is what gives CDs a shiny look. Dyes are used to create different colored **reflective** layers. The reflective layer can be blue, gold, purple, black, silver, or white.

Go Metric!

It's easy to change measurements to metric! Just use this chart.

To change	into	multiply by
inches	centimeters	2.54
inches	millimeters	25.4
feet	meters	.305
yards	meters	.914

Solving an environmental problem this big calls for lots of creative thinking. Rather than tossing your scratched CDs in the trash, **recycle** them into something new. Old CDs make great coasters and secret journals. Even the cases can be turned into stylish photo frames. Get ready to save the environment one CD at a time.

reflective — acting as a mirror

recycle — to make used items into new products

Stick 'em Up

Turn your locker from drab to fab in just a few minutes. All it takes are a couple of CD magnets and some of your favorite photos. Before long, your friends will be begging you to help them make their own.

Here's what you need:
- all-purpose glue
- 2 CDs
- tape measure
- sticky-back magnet strip
- scissors
- permanent markers (optional)

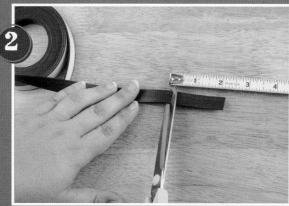

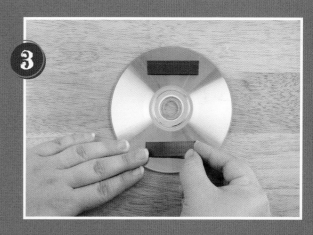

Step 1
Glue the lower halves of two CDs together with the shiny sides facing out.

Step 2
Use a tape measure to mark off two 2-inch strips of magnet. Cut magnet strips.

Step 3
Peel the backing off the magnet strips and attach to the top and bottom of one CD.

Optional
Use permanent markers to add fun designs to the CD magnet.

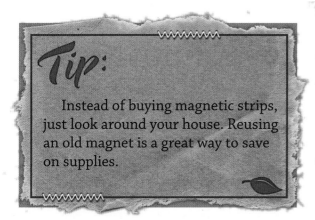

Tip:

Instead of buying magnetic strips, just look around your house. Reusing an old magnet is a great way to save on supplies.

Party Coasters

Everyone knows CDs with the latest tunes will get your party rocking. But did you know CDs can add sparkle to your table too? Just hand your guests CD coasters along with their drinks.

Here's what you need:
- 1 CD
- piece of felt at least 5 inches by 5 inches
- permanent marker
- scissors
- all-purpose glue
- small plastic gems

XXXX

Step 1
Place a CD onto a piece of felt. Trace around the CD with a marker.

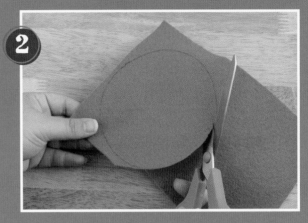

Step 2
Cut out the felt circle.

Step 3
Glue the felt onto the label side of the CD.

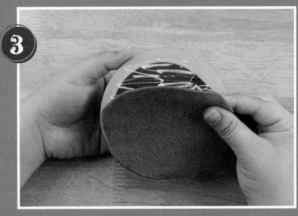

Step 4
Glue plastic gems around the outside edge of the CD.

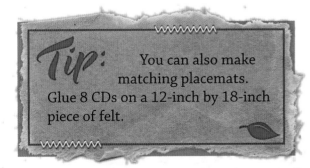

Tip: You can also make matching placemats. Glue 8 CDs on a 12-inch by 18-inch piece of felt.

Mosaic Flowerpot

Brighten your backyard with a **mosaic** flowerpot made with old CDs. Flowerpots placed throughout the garden add interest and color. Bits of broken CDs create a mirrored surface that reflects sunlight and makes your plants sparkle.

Here's what you need:
- scissors
- 3 CDs
- glue gun and hot glue
- 4 ½-inch flowerpot
- glass gems

CD SAFETY!
Safety glasses should be worn when cutting CDs. Sharp pieces can fly up.

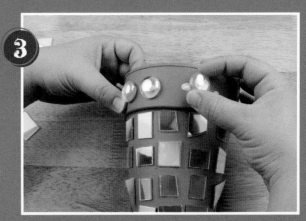

Step 1
Cut the CDs into small pieces.

Step 2
Hot glue the CD pieces onto the flowerpot. Leave a small space between each piece.

Step 3
Hot glue gems along the top edge of the pot. Allow the glue to dry before adding dirt and flowers.

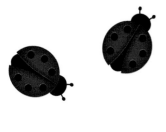

mosaic — a pattern or picture made up of small pieces of colored materials

Window Wrap

Add some sparkle to your room with a CD window **valance**. Take a plain **dowel** and add colorful ribbons and flowers to showcase your personal style. When the sun hits the CDs, your whole room will shine.

Step 1
Cut ribbon into three 18-inch strips and two 14-inch strips.

Step 2
Place CDs shiny side up on a table. Hot glue a silk flower in the center of each CD.

Step 3
Hot glue a CD to the bottom of an 18-inch strip of ribbon. Repeat with the other 18-inch strips.

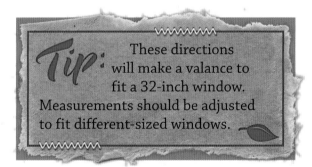

Tip: These directions will make a valance to fit a 32-inch window. Measurements should be adjusted to fit different-sized windows.

To finish this project, turn to the next page.

valance — a short curtain hung along the top edge of a window
dowel — a long, round piece of wood

Step 4
Hot glue another flowered CD 9 inches above the center of the first CD. Repeat with the other 18-inch strips.

Step 5
Hot glue a CD shiny side up on the bottom of a 14-inch strip. Repeat with the other 14-inch strip.

Step 6
Wrap the top of an 18-inch strip around the end of a wooden dowel. Glue in place. Repeat on the other end.

Step 7 *(not pictured)*
Use a tape measure to find the center of the dowel. Wrap the third 18-inch strip around the center. Glue in place.

Step 8

Center the 14-inch strips between the 18-inch strips. Glue in place.

Step 9

With an adult's help, hammer three small nails, angled up, into the wall above your window.

Step 10

Hang the valance on the nails.

Tip: If there's already a curtain rod in your window, try hanging the valance over the top of the curtains. (*shown on page 12*)

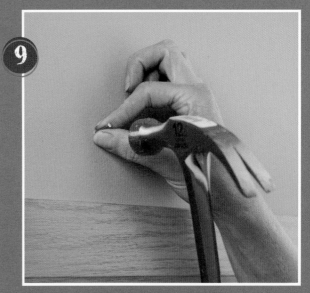

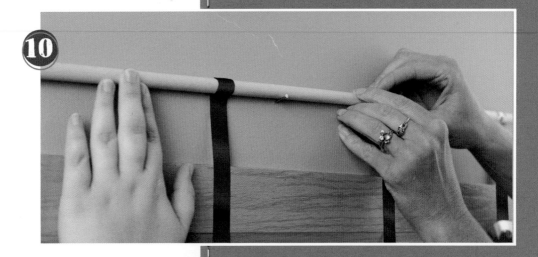

Secret Journal

Got a nosy brother who keeps trying to sneak peeks at your journal? Then you need a top-secret CD journal. This journal is kept hidden inside a CD case. Only you will know what's really inside.

Here's what you need:
- 1 piece of paper, 8.5-inch by 11-inch
- 2 CDs
- pencil
- scissors
- glue stick
- CD case

1

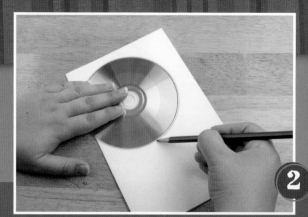

2

Step 1
Fold paper in half lenthwise.

Step 2
Place a CD on the paper so the CD edge overlaps the fold. Trace the CD on the paper, including the center hole.

Step 3
Cut out circle along the traced line. Do not cut through the fold. Cut out the center hole.

Step 4
Glue one paper circle to the shiny side of a CD.

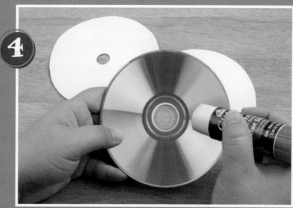

Step 5
Glue the other circle to the label of a second CD.

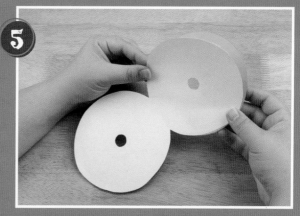

Step 6
Hide the journal in a CD case. When you're ready to write, just open the CDs and write on the paper.

Tip: Use an 11-inch by 17-inch piece of paper to create more circles and more writing space.

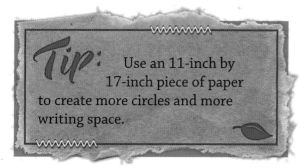

17

Catching Some Rays

A suncatcher is an ornament that reflects sunlight. Because they're made with a shiny, reflective material, CDs are natural suncatchers. Hang a few outside on a tree to make your backyard shine.

Here's what you need:

- **glue gun and hot glue**
- 4 CDs
- curling ribbon (optional)
- ruler
- permanent marker
- scissors
- fishing line or string

Step 1

Hot glue two CDs together so that the shiny sides are on the outside.

Optional

Glue curling ribbon between CDs in step 1.

Step 2

Use a ruler to mark the center of a third CD. Cut CD in half.

Step 3

Glue the two halves together with the shiny sides on the outside.

Step 4 *(not pictured)*

Repeat steps 2 and 3 with a fourth CD.

Step 5

Hot glue one of the CD halves to the full CD along the middle. Glue the second CD half to the other side. Allow glue to dry.

Step 6 *(not pictured)*

Thread fishing line or string through the center hole and tie at the top of the suncatcher.

Tip: Create several suncatchers and hang them at different levels around the yard on bushes and trees. For indoor suncatchers, hang them in windows that receive the most sun.

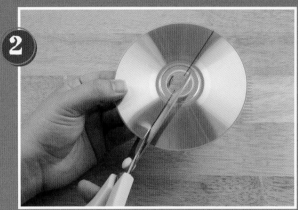

You've Been Framed

Old CDs are great for craft projects, but the reusing doesn't stop there. After all, even the packaging can be recycled into something new. A shiny CD border turns a plastic CD case into a cool stand-up frame.

Here's what you need:
- CD case
- scissors
- 1–2 CDs
- tacky glue
- transparent tape

1

2

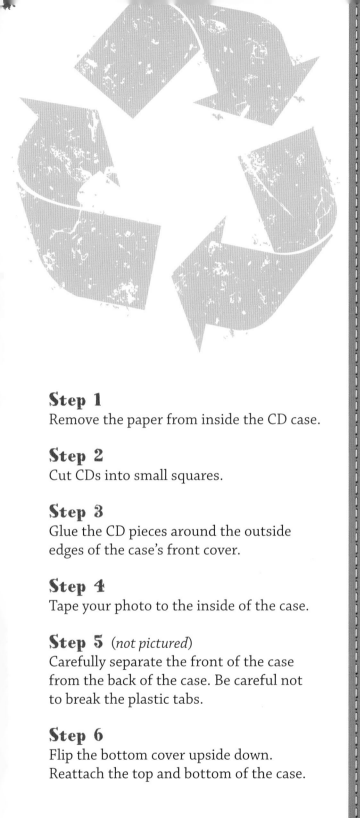

Step 1
Remove the paper from inside the CD case.

Step 2
Cut CDs into small squares.

Step 3
Glue the CD pieces around the outside edges of the case's front cover.

Step 4
Tape your photo to the inside of the case.

Step 5 *(not pictured)*
Carefully separate the front of the case from the back of the case. Be careful not to break the plastic tabs.

Step 6
Flip the bottom cover upside down. Reattach the top and bottom of the case.

> **CD SAFETY!**
> Safety glasses should be worn when cutting CDs. Sharp pieces can fly up.

Wallflower

Turn your bedroom into a beautiful garden by covering the walls with wallflowers. With some old CDs, you can create a look that's sure to brighten up your day.

Step 1
Arrange six CDs in a circle with edges overlapping. Shiny sides should face down.

Step 2
Use a marker to trace where the CDs overlap. These lines will show you where to apply the glue in step 3.

Step 3
Hot glue the CDs together in a circle. When the glue dries, flip over the CD circle so the shiny side faces up.

Step 4
Hot glue a CD shiny side up to the center of the CD circle. Flip over the CD circle so the shiny side faces down.

Step 5
Hot glue a CD to the center of the flower on the back side. This CD will help hold the flower together.

Step 6
Thread a ribbon through the center holes of two CD petals. Tie a bow at the top.

Optional
Glue plastic gems around the center CD.

Step 7 *(not pictured)*
With an adult's help, attach an adhesive wall hook to the wall. Hang CD flower on the hook.

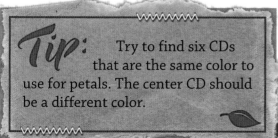

Tip: Try to find six CDs that are the same color to use for petals. The center CD should be a different color.

3

4

5

6

Time to Shine

This wall clock combines function, style, and your old CDs. You'll never again have an excuse for showing up late to class.

Here's what you need:
- 9 CDs
- permanent marker
- glue gun and hot glue
- clockworks
- 2 metal washers
- 1 AA battery

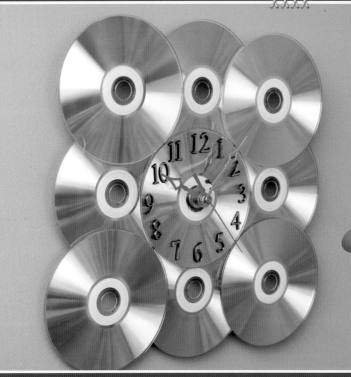

1

2

Step 1

Place one CD shiny side down on a table. Arrange four CDs shiny side down on top of the first CD.

Step 2

Use a marker to trace where the four CDs overlap the center CD. These lines will show you where to apply the glue in step 3.

Step 3

Hot glue the four CDs to the center CD. When the glue dries, flip over the CDs.

Step 4

Hot glue four CDs shiny side up around the center circle.

Step 5

Attach numbers from a clockworks set to the center CD.

Step 6

Place two metal washers over the CD hole. Attach the clockworks to the center of the CD as directed on package. Insert a battery to make the clock run.

Tip: Clockworks can be purchased at craft stores or hobby stores. You can also reuse the clockworks from an old clock.

3

4

5

6

Stamp Wrap

Give a gift as unique as your personality and help the environment at the same time. Just wrap your gift in homemade stamp wrap. With this project, you're not just reusing CDs. You're reusing lids and paper bags too.

Here's what you need:
- **permanent marker**
- **1 CD**
- **cardboard**
- **utility knife**
- **all-purpose glue**
- **screw lid**
  (like the top of a peanut butter jar)
- **scissors**
- **paper bag**
- **paintbrush**
- **acrylic paint**

1

2

Step 1
Use a marker to draw a simple design on the shiny side of a CD. You can create a cardboard stencil to trace around.

Step 2
Place the CD shiny side up on a piece of cardboard. With an adult's help, use a utility knife to cut the design into the CD. You will want to go over the design several times to create deep grooves.

Step 3
Turn the CD over. Glue a screw lid to the center of the CD.

Step 4
Cut out the bottom and one side of a paper bag so the bag lays flat.

Step 5 *(not pictured)*
Brush a thin layer of acrylic paint over your CD design.

Step 6
Press the CD paint side down onto the paper bag. Press down firmly for a few seconds. Carefully lift the CD so the paint doesn't smear.

Step 7
Repeat step 6 until paper is covered with stamps. Let paint dry before wrapping a gift.

Tip: Use the CD stamp to decorate a T-shirt or canvas bag.

Green Crafting Facts

🐞 CDs are considered class 7 recyclables. Class 7 plastics are the hardest to recycle.

🐞 Scientists believe it will take more than 1 million years for a CD to completely break down in a landfill.

🐞 Recycled CDs are used to make auto parts, street lights, and office equipment.

🐞 In 1983, 800,000 CDs were sold in the United States. More than 400 million CDs were sold in 2008.

🐞 Still have leftover CDs after making all the crafts in this book? You can mail them to an organization that recycles CDs. For more information, check out The Compact Disc Recycling Center of America online.

Glossary

dowel (DOW-ul) — a long, round piece of wood

environment (in-VY-ruhn-muhnt) — the natural world of the land, water, and air

landfill (LAND-fill) — an area where garbage is stacked and covered with dirt

mosaic (moh-ZAY-ik) — a pattern or picture made up of small pieces of colored materials

ornament (OR-nuh-muhnt) — a small, attractive object used as a decoration

recycle (ree-SYE-kuhl) — to make used items into new products; people can recycle items such as rubber, glass, plastic, and aluminum.

reflective (ri-FLEK-tiv) — acting as a mirror

suncatcher (SUHN-ka-chur) — a decorative piece of glass or other shiny material that is hung in a window to reflect the sun's rays

valance (VAL-uhns) — a short curtain hung along the top edge of a window

XXXX

Read More

Craig, Rebecca. *Gorgeous Gifts: Use Recycled Materials to Make Cool Crafts*. Ecocrafts. Boston: Kingfisher, 2007.

Rodger, Ellen. *Recycling Waste*. Saving Our World. Tarrytown, N.Y.: Marshall Cavendish Benchmark, 2008.

Ross, Kathy. *Earth-Friendly Crafts: Clever Ways to Reuse Everyday Items*. Minneapolis: Millbrook Press, 2009.

Internet Sites

FactHound offers a safe, fun way to find Internet sites related to this book. All of the sites on FactHound have been researched by our staff.

Here's all you do:

Visit *www.facthound.com*

FactHound will fetch
the best sites for you!

Index

About the Author

Carol Sirrine is a former elementary classroom, music, and art teacher. In 1988, she founded ArtStart, an organization that combines learning in the arts with environmental stewardship. ArtStart's ArtScraps, located in St. Paul, Minnesota, combines waste management with art making. In a unique partnership with businesses and manufacturers, ArtScraps collects scraps, overstock, factory rejects, and other items normally destined for the landfill. These products are made available to teachers, parents, artists, Scout leaders, and day-care providers.